The Ultimate Llama & Alpaca Book

Learn more about your favorite camelids.

Jenny Kellett

Copyright © 2021 by Jenny Kellett

The Ultimate Llama & Alpaca Book
www.bellanovabooks.com

All rights reserved. No part of this book may be reproduced in any form by any electronic or mechanical means including photocopying, recording, or information storage and retrieval without permission in writing from the author.

ISBN: 9798531913845
Imprint: Independently published

Contents

Introduction 4
Facts - The Basics 6
Species 22
    Vicuña 22
    Guanaco 26
    Alpacas 30
    Domesticated llamas.............. 34
From Birth to Adulthood 36
Their Daily Lives 48
Llamas and Us 60
More Fun Facts 68
Llama Quiz 76
    Answers 81
Wordsearch 82
Sources 84

Introduction

There are few animals more adorable than llamas and alpacas. Their soft, fluffy coats and bright, wide eyes are just some of the reasons why so many people have fallen in love with these beautiful creatures.

In this book we will take a look at llamas, as well as their close relatives the alpaca, vicuña and guanaco. How can you tell them apart? Where do they live? And much more.

You'll be bursting full of new knowledge, which you can test in the quiz at the end of the book.

Are you ready? *Let's go!*

Llamas & Alpacas – The Basics

What are they and where do they live?

The scientific name for a llama is *Lama glama.*

• • •

Llamas and alpacas are domesticated animals, like cats and dogs, and have been used by Andean cultures for food and as transport animals for over 500 years. They evolved from vicuña and guanaco, which remain wild and undomesticated today.

A wild guanaco.

Llamas are **camelids**, which puts them in the same family as camels and alpacas.

• • •

Camelids are **even-toed ungulates**, which is a category of animal that also includes cows, pigs, and deer.

• • •

They are also classified as **mammals**, meaning that they give birth to live young and feed them milk.

The term **lama** is often used to describe all members of the camelid family, although most people just think it is llama misspelled.

• • •

Llamas haven't always lived in South America. It is thought that they originated in central North America 40 million years ago and only migrated to South America three million years ago.

A llama on top of Chimborazo volcano, the highest peak in Ecuador.

Llamas in Bolivia.

There are an estimated seven million llamas and alpacas living in South America.

• • •

Llamas are very peaceful animals and are rarely violent. However, if they are angry or distressed they may spit at you!

• • •

Llamas live to be around 20 years old. However, some live until they are 30.

Llamas and alpacas look very similar, and that's because they are! They both belong to the group called **lamoids**. Also in the lamoid family are vicuñas and guanacos, which we will take a closer look at soon.

• • •

Fully-grown domesticated llamas weigh between 130 and 200 kg (290 and 440 lb) and reach a height of 1.7 to 1.8 m (5'7" to 5'11").

• • •

As well as being bred for transport, llamas have a soft undercoat, which is used for making clothes and handicrafts. Their coarser outercoat is used for rugs, ropes, and wall hangings.

Llamas can't be ridden by humans, except sometimes by small children.

...

Llamas can run very fast — up to 40 mph (64km/h), but usually only if they are trying to escape danger.

...

Llamas and alpacas are both very sociable, but llamas are slightly more independent than alpacas.

A group of domesticated alpacas being walked.

Llamas only have teeth in the bottom front of their mouths. On the top, it is just rubbery. They also have molars at the back to help with chewing.

Llamas have been imported into the USA and Canada since the 1800s, and there are now over 150,000 llamas there. Some are kept as pets, but most are bred for their fiber.

• • •

Llamas also live happily in Australia. There are around 3,500 living there.

• • •

Llamas's feet have a unique structure that keeps them stable while walking on rocky terrain. They have two toes (rather than hooves), each with a toenail and a soft, leathery pad. Their soft feet cause minimal damage to the environment.

Species: Vicuña
Scientific name: *Vicugna vicugna*

Vicuñas are one of two species of **wild lamoid**, which live in the very high alpine regions of the Andes. They live in family groups, which usually consist of one male and up to 15 females, as well as the young.

They are quite small compared to other members of the lamoid family and have a long woolly coat, which is brown on the back and white on the throat and chest.

The vicuña is the national symbol of Peru and you will see it on the country's coat of arms.

A group of vicuñas.

A wild vicuña in the desert.

Although most vicuñas live in Peru, they can also be found in northwestern Argentina, Bolivia, and northern Chile.

Their coats produce fine, soft wool, which is very expensive as they can only be shorn once every three years. It is deemed so special, that the Inca forbade anyone except for royalty from wearing clothing made from vicuña wool.

Vicuñas are very valued by the Peruvian people and are protected by law. However, in the 1970s, the vicuña was listed as endangered as they were heavily hunted. In 1974 there were only 6,000 vicuñas left — but now, after new laws came into place, there are over 350,000!

Vicuñas are very shy animals. They have great hearing, so are easily disturbed by nearby humans or predators.

Species: Guanaco
Scientific name: *Lama guanicoe*

The guanaco is the other species of wild lamoid. Unlike the vicuña, they live in the lower alpine regions of the Andes. They are very closely related to the llama and are much larger than vicuñas. They are one of the largest land mammals living in South America.

Guanacos live in Peru, Bolivia, and Chile. There are populations of guanaco living in the Atacama desert, where in some areas, it hasn't rained for over 50 years. However, the nearby coastline helps to create a water vapor fog over some areas of the desert that keeps cacti and succulent plants alive, which the guanacos then eat.

A wild guanaco.

A female guanaco and her chulengo.
Photo by Miranda Salzgeber on Unsplash

Like the vicuña, they have very beautiful, soft fur (similar to cashmere), which is very expensive. They have grey faces and small, straight ears.

There are an estimated 400,000-600,000 guanacos living in South America. However, several populations of guanaco are listed as a threatened species, and there is a risk they will become extinct. In Peru, for example, there are only around 3,500 guanacos left. And in Paraguay, only 100.

There are also around 300 guanacos living in zoos across the USA, but otherwise they have not been domesticated.

Species: Alpaca (Suri & Huacaya)

Scientific name: *Vicugna pacos*

The *vicugna pacos* species is made up of the two breeds of alpaca: Suri and Huacaya. They live on the Altiplano plateau of the Andes mountain range, at around 4,000m elevation.

Approximately 90 percent of all alpacas are huacaya alpacas and more than half of the global population of alpacas lives in Peru.

Alpacas and llamas are often confused, but the easiest way to tell them apart is by their size — alpacas are much smaller than llamas.

A huacaya alpaca in New Zealand.

A suri alpaca.

While llamas were bred to be working animals, alpacas were bred for their fur (known as fiber), which is similar to sheep's wool, only finer.

Alpaca fiber comes in 22 natural colors and is popular for making items such as ponchos, blankets, and scarves.

Suri and huacaya alpacas look very similar — when they are born they weigh and look the same. However, the main difference is in their coats. Huacaya fiber is spongier and curlier, while the suri's is softer, longer, and straighter — almost like dreadlocks.

Species: Domesticated Llamas

Scientific name: *Lama glama*

The domestic llama is just that — domesticated. They are calm, friendly and spend most of their lives working up and down the mountains. Recently they have also been used as therapy animals in nursing homes and rehabilitation centers.

Llamas are almost twice the size of alpacas and have longer heads and tall, curved ears.

Their coats can be a wide range of different colors, even spotted, and although their fiber is used to make clothing and other goods, it is not as popular as the alpacas, which are slightly softer.

From birth to adulthood

Let's learn more about the early life of lamoids.

Baby llamas, alpacas, and vicuñas are called **crias**, which came from the Spanish word for baby.

• • •

Baby guanacos are called **chulengos**.

• • •

Juvenile llamas are called **tuis** in the local Quechua language.

Llamas that have been weaned but are still under one year old are called **weanlings**, whereas a llama aged between one and two is called a **yearling**.

• • •

The mother of a cria is called a **dam**.

• • •

The father of a cria is called a **sire**.

• • •

< A young Peruvian girl with an alpaca yearling.

When a female llama gives birth, all the other female llamas in the group gather around her to protect the newborn from predators.

• • •

Llamas give birth standing up.

• • •

To help protect the newborns from harsh weather, llamas usually give birth in the morning when it is warmer.

• • •

The **gestation period** (how long a female is pregnant) is 11.5 months.

A young white cria.

Two young crias.

A young guanaco is called a **chulengo**. Male chulengos are chased off by the dominant male in their herd when they reach around one year old.

Crias can walk around and suckle milk within an hour of being born.

• • •

Llamas usually give birth to only one cria at a time — twins are very rare.

• • •

When they are born, crias weigh between 20-35 lb (9-16kg).

• • •

Male uncastrated llamas and alpacas are called **studs** (or machos in Spanish), whereas castrated ones are called **geldings**.

Female llamas and alpacas are called **hembras** in Spanish or simply 'females' in English.

• • •

Female alpacas are usually first bred when they are 18 months old, while llamas are bred between 14-24 months old.

• • •

It is possible to cross-breed alpacas and llamas. The resulting animal is called a **huarizo**.

A vicuña and her cria >

Wild guanacos in Patagonia.

Llama's Daily Lives

The daily life and behavior of llamas and alpacas largely depends on whether they are domesticated or not. So let's take a look at what it's like to be a lamoid!

Llamas are very sociable animals and live together in groups called **herds**.

. . .

They are smart and can learn simple commands from humans quickly.

A young alpaca in the snow.

A domesticated llama.

Llamas can carry 25-30% of their body weight over long distances when using packs, which makes them very useful for helping humans carry goods up and down the steep Andes mountains.

• • •

Llamas are **herbivores**, meaning they don't eat meat. However, they are not particularly fussy eaters and most domesticated llamas will eat special feed that their owners give to them. Llamas eat between 2-4 percent of their body weight each day.

• • •

Wild guanaco and vicuña eat mostly grasses and other easy-to-find food.

In a herd of llamas, each member has their own social rank. A llama can move up or down the social rank by picking fights with others.

• • •

Llamas have five different speeds (or gaits): walk, pace, trot, gallop, and pronk. **Pronking** is when usually juvenile llamas and alpacas jump stiffly up into the air in a playful way.

• • •

When llamas are scared, uncomfortable, or stressed they make a sound called **humming**.

A Peruvian alpaca.

A working llama in Peru.

Llamas will often engage in **rolling**, which involves rolling around on their backs side to side. They do this to create air pockets in their coats to help keep them warm.

• • •

Llamas are very talkative! They communicate with each other through different ear, tail, and body language as well as a range of sounds.

• • •

There aren't different breeds of llamas or alpacas, however, breeders will classify them into different groups based on their coat type.

Like camels, llamas don't need to drink very often as they can store it. However, they do drink more in the summer months and can be often seen refreshing themselves near a lake or stream.

• • •

Llamas's biggest threats are mountain lions, coyotes, and ocelots.

• • •

If a llama can't escape a predator, it may use a powerful kick to fight it off.

Llamas don't need much land to be happy and have enough food. One acre (0.4 hectares) of land is enough to sustain four llamas (or 10 alpacas!).

• • •

In the wild, male llamas will stand at a high point to look out for predators and protect the females in the herd.

• • •

In the Andes, you will often see pack trains of hundreds of llamas transporting goods along the rocky terrain.

Llamas and Us

How do llamas fit into the human world? What is their future?

Fortunately, most lamoids have a safe future. Only the guanaco is endangered.

• • •

Llamas and alpacas are an important part of many traditional South American cultures. The pre-Incan civilization **the Moche people** would offer llamas in the burials of important people to help in their afterlife. And the Inca deity **Urcuchillay** was depicted as a multi-colored llama.

A llama in Bolivia.

A young cria being carried by a local Peruvian.

Llamas were a very important part of the growth of the Inca Empire, as the wheel had not yet been invented and so llamas were crucial for carrying supplies.

• • •

Every December 9th in the USA is **National Llama Day**! On this day, llama lovers celebrate the majestic creature — not only for its cuteness, but for all the work it does for mankind.

• • •

Llamas have been a huge part of popular culture for the last few years.

The video game 'Fortnite' started a llama-mania trend in 2018 that triggered a huge demand for llama-related goods. Now, toy brands all over the world have created their own versions of llama and alpaca toys. You can even buy a llama Slinky!

...

I bet you're wondering whether you can have an alpaca or llama as a pet? Well, they actually make great pets! But of course they need a lot more work and care than a dog or cat. They also only like to be in a pair or as a group.

Llamas are often decorated in bright colors by their owners.

A young alpaca.

The 2000 movie *The Emperor's New Groove,* features an Incan emperor that gets turned into a llama.

• • •

In 1998 the first camel and llama hybrid was born. Called a **cama**, the animal was bred to try and increase wool production. As of 2008, five camas had been born.

• • •

If you want to spend time with a llama or alpaca, there are lots of places around the USA, Australia and Europe where you can take them for walks, pet them or feed them. They are very friendly!

Other Fun Facts

From the wild to the wonderful.

Llamas have attached tongues, which means they can't stick them out more than 13mm (1⁄2 inch).

• • •

Llama poop is almost odorless! Because of this, it is a popular fertilizer.

• • •

Llamas have three parts to their stomachs: the rumen, omasum, and abomasum.

A young alpaca.

Like cows, llamas must regurgitate their food before swallowing it again to fully digest it.

• • •

Llamas and alpacas have been used as guard animals since the 1980s. They are used to protect other livestock such as sheep from predators.

Although llamas can carry huge weights, they know their limits! If you give them too much to carry, they will lie down or simply refuse to carry it.

• • •

Llamas have a similar metabolic system to humans, so scientists are using them to test out new treatments for diabetics.

• • •

Llama hiking has become a popular trend in countries outside of South America, such as the USA and the UK.

Research has shown that kids are likely to walk twice as far if they are accompanied by a llama, which is great for improving their health.

• • •

When a llama has big, curved ears in the shape of a banana, the official term used by biologists is **'banana ears'**.

• • •

Alpaca and llama fiber is hypoallergenic, which makes it a great material for bedding and clothing.

If you meet a llama, you should only pet it on its back or neck, as this is where they like it best. It is also where their hair is the thickest.

• • •

When llamas are being transported in a vehicle they will usually lie down.

• • •

Alpacas produce the strongest animal fiber in the world, after mohair.

< **Alpacas in Peru.**

The red blood cells in camelids are oval-shaped.

• • •

Llamas eyes can look in different directions at the same time!

• • •

Llamas and alpacas are 'communal poopers'. This means that members of a herd usually all go to the toilet in the same place. Their poops look like black jelly beans.

• • •

Guanacos have 4 times as many red blood cells in their blood as humans, which helps them to survive at higher elevations where oxygen levels are low.

A suri alpaca.

Llama & Alpaca *Quiz*

Now test your knowledge in our quiz! Answers are on page 81.

1. Can you name the four different species of lamoid?

2. How many llamas and alpacas live in South America?

3. Which is the smallest member of the lamoid family?

4. What are baby guanacos called?

5. What are the two types of alpacas?

A shorn alpaca.

6. What is the easiest way to tell llamas and alpacas apart?

7. How many different colors can alpaca fiber come in?

8. What are baby llamas, alpacas and vicuñas called?

9. What is the mother of a cria called?

10. How do llamas give birth?

11. How long is the gestation period for lamoids?

12. Most lamoids give birth to twins. True or false?

13. If a llama and an alpaca are cross-bred, what is the resulting animal called?

14. What is a group of llamas called?

15. Llamas and alpacas are herbivores. True or false?

16. Why do llamas sometimes roll around on the ground?

17. When is National Llama Day?

18. What is strange about llamas' tongues?

19. Why does llama poop make such a great fertilizer?

20. Why do guanacos have so many red blood cells?

Answers:

1. Vicuña, guanaco, llama and alpaca.
2. Seven million.
3. The vicuña.
4. Chulengos.
5. Suri and Huacaya.
6. Alpacas are much smaller than llamas.
7. 22.
8. Crias.
9. A dam.
10. Standing up.
11. 11.5 months.
12. False. Twins are very rare.
13. A huarizo.
14. A herd.
15. True.
16. To create air pockets in their coats to keep them warm.
17. December 9th.
18. They are attached so they can't stick them out very far.
19. It is almost odorless!
20. So that they can survive in high altitudes, where oxygen levels are low.

Llama & Alpaca
WORDSEARCH

F	G	H	J	R	T	Y	P	I	U	T	R
T	L	R	W	G	F	S	A	N	B	C	S
R	A	R	E	A	L	P	A	C	A	Y	V
E	M	Q	D	S	A	H	G	F	N	T	I
E	O	G	Y	R	E	Q	F	G	D	E	C
B	I	H	L	A	K	J	C	N	E	V	U
N	D	G	S	L	F	R	W	R	S	C	N
S	O	U	T	H	A	M	E	R	I	C	A
W	A	S	U	T	R	M	W	D	F	A	A
D	A	T	A	C	A	M	A	N	G	F	C
F	F	D	J	G	R	Y	T	W	A	C	V
G	A	G	U	A	N	A	C	O	M	N	B

A young alpaca.

Can you find all the words below in the wordsearch puzzle on the left?

LLAMA   ALPACA   GUANACO

VICUNA   ATACAMA   ANDES

SOUTH AMERICA   CRIA   LAMOID

Sources

A-Z, Animals, Animal 10s, Most Endangered, Highest Jumpers, Longest Living, Endangered Change, and Unusual Habits et al. 2021. "Amazing Facts About Llamas | Onekindplanet Animal Education & Facts". Onekindplanet. *https://onekindplanet.org/animal/llama/.*

"Llama - Wikipedia". 2021. En.Wikipedia.Org. *https://en.wikipedia.org/wiki/Llama#Classification.*

"Vicuña - Wikipedia". 2021. En.Wikipedia.Org. *https://en.wikipedia.org/wiki/Vicu%C3%B1a.*

"Alpaca - Wikipedia". 2018. En.Wikipedia.Org. *https://en.wikipedia.org/wiki/Alpaca.*

"24 Fun Facts About Llamas". 2021. Thoughtco. *https://www.thoughtco.com/fun-facts-about-llamas-3880940.*

"Five Cool Things About Llamas". 2012. Animal Connection. *https://blogs.oregonstate.edu/animalconnection/2012/01/19/five-cool-things-about-llamas/.*

"Llama Hiking - Wikipedia". 2021. En.Wikipedia.Org. *https://en.wikipedia.org/wiki/Llama_hiking.*

2021. Ag.Ndsu.Edu. *https://www.ag.ndsu.edu/stutsmancountyextension/news-articles/llama-terminology.*

"A Guide To Llamas, Alpacas, Guanacos, And Vicuñas". 2021. Thoughtco. *https://www.thoughtco.com/guide-to-llamas-alpacas-guanacos-and-vincunas-1619852.*

"Llama Fun Facts – Mtn Peaks Therapy Llamas & Alpacas". 2021. Rojothellama.Com. *https://rojothellama.com/llama-fun-facts/.*

"Llama | National Geographic". 2021. Animals. *https://www.nationalgeographic.com/animals/mammals/facts/llama-1.*

We hope you learnt some awesome facts about llamas and alpacas! What was your favourite? Tell us in a review on Amazon.

Follow us at www.bellanovabooks.com for the latest animal book releases.

Printed in Great Britain
by Amazon